A Home
for Me

Mobile Home

Lola M. Schaefer

Heinemann Library
Chicago, Illinois

©2003 Reed Educational & Professional Publishing
Published by Heinemann Library,
an imprint of Reed Educational & Professional Publishing
Chicago, IL

Customer Service 888-454-2279
Visit our website at www.heinemannlibrary.com

Designed by Sue Emerson, Heinemann Library
Printed and bound in the United States by Lake Book Manufacturing, Inc.

07 06 05 04 03
10 9 8 7 6 5 4 3 2 1

Library of Congress Cataloging-in-Publication Data
Lola M. Schaefer
     Mobile Home / Lola M. Schaefer.
        p. cm. — (A Home for Me)
Includes index.
Contents: What is a mobile home?—What do mobile homes look like?—How big are mobile homes?—How many rooms are in a mobile home?—Where do people talk and play in a mobile home?—Where do people cook in a mobile home?—Where do people sleep in a mobile home?—Where do people bathe in a mobile home?—What other rooms might be in a mobile home?—Mobile home map quiz—Mobile home picture glossary.
     ISBN: 1-4034-0263-9 (HC), 1-4034-0486-0 (Pbk.)
     1. Mobile homes—Juvenile literature. Mobile home living—Juvenile literature. [1. Mobile homes. 2. Mobile home living.] I. Title. II. Series: Schaefer, Lola M., 1950– . Home for me.
     TX1106.S33 2002
     643.2—dc21

                          2001008146

Acknowledgments
The author and publishers are grateful to the following for permission to reproduce copyright material:
pp. 4, 5, 8, 9 Douglas Keister; pp. 6, 7, 12, 13, 14, 15, 16, 18, 19, 21 Greg Williams/Heinemann Library; p. 17 William Hart/Stone/Getty Images; p. 20 D. Yeske/Visuals Unlimited; p. 23 (row 1, L-R) William Hart/Stone/Getty Images, Greg Williams/Heinemann Library, Robert Lifson/Heinemann Library; p. 23 (row 2, L-R) Greg Williams/Heinemann Library, Jeff Greenberg/Visuals Unlimited, Robert Lifson/Heinemann Library; p. 23 (row 3, L-R) Robert Lifson/Heinemann Library, Heinemann Library; back cover Greg Williams/Heinemann Library

Cover photograph by Greg Williams/Heinemann Library
Photo research by Amor Montes de Oca
Special thanks to our models, the Ellison family, and to Carefree Sales for the use of their location.

Every effort has been made to contact copyright holders of any material reproduced in this book. Any omissions will be rectified in subsequent printings if notice is given to the publisher.

Special thanks to our advisory panel for their help in the preparation of this book:

Eileen Day, Preschool teacher
Chicago, IL

Ellen Dolmetsch,
Library Media Specialist
Wilmington, DE

Kathleen Gilbert,
Second Grade Teacher
Round Rock, TX

Sandra Gilbert,
Library Media Specialist
Houston, TX

Angela Leeper,
Educational Consultant
North Carolina Department
of Public Instruction
Raleigh, NC

Pam McDonald,
Reading Support Specialist
Winter Springs, FL

Melinda Murphy,
Library Media Specialist
Houston, TX

Some words are shown in bold, **like this.**
You can find them in the picture glossary on page 23.

Contents

What Is a Mobile Home?

A mobile home is a house that moves.

A large truck can pull it from place to place.

Some mobile homes have wheels underneath.

The wheels can't roll when the house is parked.

What Do Mobile Homes Look Like?

Mobile homes look like long **rectangles.**

They are painted light colors.

Mobile homes have doors and windows.

Sometimes they even have a **garage**.

How Big Are Mobile Homes?

Some mobile homes are as wide as two buses.

Small mobile homes are about
as big as one bus.

How Many Rooms Are in a Mobile Home?

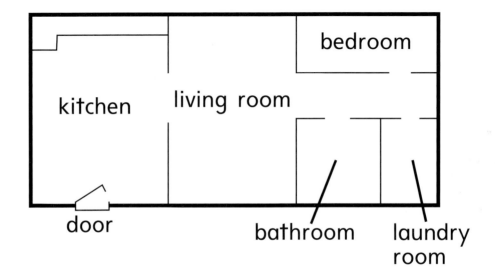

kitchen

living room

bedroom

door

bathroom

laundry room

A small mobile home may have four or five rooms.

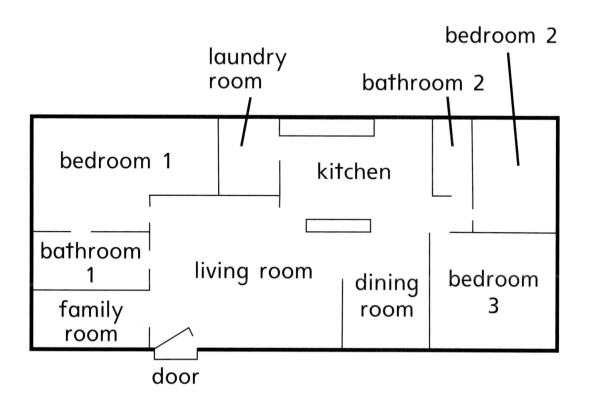

A large mobile home can have more than nine rooms.

Where Do People Talk and Play?

People talk and play in the living room.

A living room has a sofa, chairs, tables, and lamps.

People can play games in the living room.

They can read, too.

Where Do People Cook and Eat?

People cook in a kitchen.

Kitchens in mobile homes have refrigerators and **stoves**.

Some people eat their meals in the kitchen.

Other people eat their meals in the dining room.

Where Do People Sleep?

People sleep in bedrooms in a mobile home.

Bedrooms have beds, **dressers,** and closets.

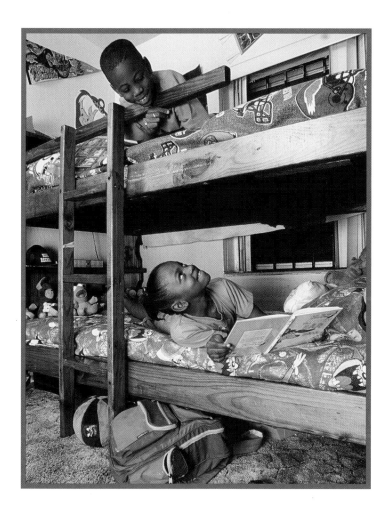

Sometimes children have **bunkbeds** in their bedroom.

Two people can sleep in a bunkbed.

Where Do People Take Baths?

Mobile homes have bathrooms.

Most bathrooms have a sink,
a toilet, and a shower.

Many mobile home bathrooms
have bathtubs.

Sometimes the bathtubs are
very big!

Where Do People Wash Their Clothes?

Some mobile homes have a **washing machine** and a **dryer**.

They can be in a closet or a laundry room.

Other mobile homes do not have a washing machine or a dryer.

Then, people wash their clothes at a **laundry**.

Map Quiz

What is the room next to the kitchen in this mobile home?

What is the room across from the bathroom?

Look for the answers on page 24.

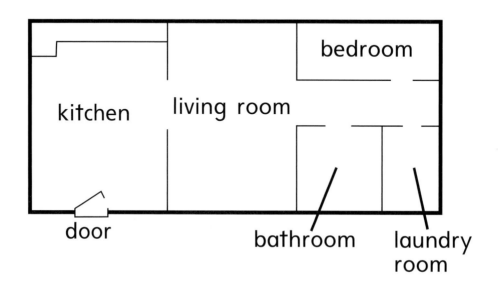

kitchen

living room

bedroom

door

bathroom

laundry room

22

Picture Glossary

bunkbed
page 17

garage
page 7

stove
page 14

dresser
page 16

laundry
page 21

washing machine
pages 20, 21

dryer
pages 20, 21

rectangle
page 6

23

Note to Parents and Teachers

Reading for information is an important part of a child's literacy development. Learning begins with a question about something. Help children think of themselves as investigators and researchers by encouraging their questions about the world around them. Each chapter in this book begins with a question. Read the question together. Look at the pictures. Talk about what you think the answer might be. Then read the text to find out if your predictions were correct. Think of other questions you could ask about the topic, and discuss where you might find the answers. Use the two simple maps on pages 10 and 11 to introduce children to basic map-reading skills. After discussing the maps, help children draw their own map of a familiar place, such as their room. Assist children in using the picture glossary and the index to practice new vocabulary and research skills.

Index

Answers to quiz on page 22

The living room is next to the kitchen.

The bedroom is across from the bathroom.